# VICTORIAN AND EDWARDIAN
# DUNDEE AND BROUGHTY FERRY
## FROM RARE PHOTOGRAPHS

# VICTORIAN AND EDWARDIAN
# DUNDEE and BROUGHTY FERRY
## FROM RARE PHOTOGRAPHS

**RAYMOND LAMONT-BROWN**

AND

**PETER ADAMSON**

FOREWORD

BY

RON THOMPSON

Published on behalf of the Dundee Museums and Art Galleries

by

ALVIE PUBLICATIONS ST ANDREWS

Peter Adamson dedicates this book to Kirsty, Elaine and Calum.
Raymond Lamont-Brown dedicates this book to his dear friends the Ireland Family.

First published in 1981 by
Alvie Publications
52 Buchanan Gardens
St Andrews KY16 9LX

ISBN 0 9506200 2 5

Printed in Scotland by
Spectrum Printing Company
Burlington Street
Edinburgh

# Contents

# ACKNOWLEDGEMENTS

The authors would like to thank Mr. James D. Boyd, Chief Officer of the Dundee Museums and Art Galleries, and Miss Janice Blair, Assistant Keeper Local History, for their co-operation with the project, and their assistance in the writing of the captions for the photographs.

All the photographs herein, except for the plates now mentioned, are the property of the Dundee Museums and Art Galleries.

2. Reproduced by kind permission of Mr J. Blyth, Newton of Falkland, Fife.
3. Reproduced by kind permission of the Rt. Hon. the Lord Home of the Hirsel.
23. University of St Andrews.
64, 67, 68, 69, 70, 135-139. The Valentine Collection, University of St. Andrews.

# FOREWORD

By Ron Thompson

FEW people in California have ever wanted to emigrate to Dundee. But Barbara Quinn of Santa Rosa, spending her first morning in Scotland atop The Law, stared down at the city dropping gently from her feet, then announced slowly—'You know, I could sure fall for this place. It has real character. There is a sense of great experience and history here which I find almost overwhelming.'

It is precisely for these reasons that I have never wanted to leave Dundee—not even for California! Here is a city which, in the parlance of my own profession, has always been 'a good story'. It has endured the pain and penalty of industrial and social change over many centuries and in the process shaped a people who embody the very qualities of resilience and humour necessary for such survival.

This, of course, is why the authors have chosen Dundee and Broughty Ferry as the subject of their latest dip into Scotland's past. There is much grist here for the mill, enough certainly to sustain their decision to launch a third book in this series of photographic reconstructions, the earliest volumes having dealt with Fife and the Borders.

In the pages that follow Peter Adamson, with his eye for a picture, and Raymond Lamont-Brown, with his feel for a word, have once again interlocked their talents to give us a highly evocative insight into the way Dundee was during the Victorian and Edwardian reigns. They have done so with the use of photographs which are truly remarkable works of art, taken at a time when colour-work and the three dimensional snapshot were well beyond the imagination of man. And yet, the emergence of these sophisticated processes—as with so many other scientific advances—serves not to devalue the product of earlier equipment, but rather to enhance the quality and highlight the skill of the prototype.

Photographs, we will all agree, are the most wonderful things and yet most of us now take them for granted. They allow you to look at people and places and objects which you could not possibly have seen for yourself. They give authentic shape to history and heritage. Only by knowing what has gone before can we reach a fuller understanding of what is taking place at the present. That is what I believe this book achieves in a most entertaining and enjoyable fashion.

May I say, in conclusion, how glad I am that the authors have included Broughty Ferry in this work. It was there, at the Castle, that my mother first met my father when he was serving as an army bugler just after the First World War. And, what is more, I have an old photograph to prove it!

1.     Photographer Sandon Perkins on the bridge of the vessel *Morning* off Dundee in 1906. Perkins, one time manager of
the Theatre Royal, Dundee, sailed aboard the *Morning* in 1906 as a passenger and took a reported 600 still pictures of
whaling activities together with some cine film.

# INTRODUCING VICTORIAN AND EDWARDIAN DUNDEE AND BROUGHTY FERRY

GEORGINA Charlotte Augusta Alexandrina Victoria, daughter of Prince Edward, Duke of Kent, and niece of King William IV had been proclaimed Queen from an open window in St James's Palace on June 21st, 1837. Seven years later her subjects in Dundee caught their first glimpse of her, then aged 25. The occasion was a trip from London in the royal yacht *Victoria and Albert, en route* for Blair Athol. In the party with Queen Victoria and Prince Albert was Albert Edward, Prince of Wales, Victoria, Princess Royal, the Hon. Charlotte Stuart, Viscountess Canning, eldest daughter of Lord Stuart de Rothsay and Maid of Honour, Lady Caroline Cocks. Lord Liverpool, and the Foreign Secretary, Lord Aberdeen, came too with Victoria's physician Sir James Clark. Sir Robert Peel, the Prime Minister, was to have been of the party, but his daughter was taken ill.

In her personal journal, under the date Wednesday, September 11th, 1844, Victoria recorded her impressions of Dundee:

'At six o'clock we inquired and heard that we were in the port of Dundee. Albert saw our other gentleman, who had had a very bad passage. Tuesday night they had a dreadful storm. Dundee is a very large place, and the port is large and open; the situation of the town is very fine, but the town itself is not so. The Provost and people had come on board, and wanted us to land later, but we got this satisfactorily arranged. At half-past eight we got into our barge with Vicky, and our ladies and gentlemen. The sea was bright and blue; the boat danced along beautifully. We had about a quarter of a mile row.

'A staircase, covered with red cloth, was arranged for us to land upon, and there was a great many people; but everything was so well managed that all crowding was avoided, and only the Magistrates were below the platform where the people were. Albert walked up the steps with me, I holding his arm and Vicky his hand, amid the loud cheers of the people, all the way to the carriage, our dear Vicky behaving like a grown-up person—not put out, nor frightened, nor nervous. We got into our postchaise, and at the same time Renwick *(the footman)* took Vicky up in his arms and put her in the next carriage with her governess and nurse.

'There was a great crowd in Dundee but everything was very well managed, and there would have been no crowding at all, had not, as usual, about twenty people begun to run along with the carriage, and thus forced a number of others to follow. About three miles beyond Dundee we stopped at the gate of Lord Camperdown's place: here a triumphal arch had been erected, and Lady Camperdown and Lady Duncan and her little boy, with others, were all waiting to welcome us, and were very civil and kind. The little boy, beautifully dressed in the Highland dress, was carried to Vicky, and gave her a basket with fruit and flowers.'

To this James Thomson, the Dundee historian, was able in 1847 to add more on Victoria's visit.

'By five o'clock, the town was astir, and carriages were rolling in from the surrounding country in all directions. Thousands of people were parading in the streets, examining the devices with which the more loyal of the inhabitants had adorned their houses. There was a meeting of Magistrates and Council at six o'clock, who, along with the public bodies of the neighbouring towns were all on the quay ready to receive Her Majesty by seven o'clock. The Royal Yacht, which contained the whole cause of the preparations, was lying in singular

9

quietness, when contrasted with the activity ashore. The uncertain element on which she rode was calm as a lake while the land was changing its aspect with every humour of the holiday crowd. At the harbour, preparations on a grand scale had been made for the landing. Some of the finest vessels were ranged along the quay, with their yards manned by seamen in blue jackets and white trousers. The Sixtieth Rifles were drawn up in double column from the Royal carriage along the line of procession. The upper end of the broad middle quay was occupied by a splended triumphal arch *(see plate 42)*, eighty feet across, consisting of three archways, closed by ornamental gates, and embellished with appropriate emblems and mottoes. From the sides of the arch, running down each side of the quay were platforms, containing hundreds of spectators, between which the Royal carriage and Suite passed and deafening cheers and waving of handkerchiefs, until it arrived at the arch, whose doors were thrown open, and the Queen was received on the outside by the escort of Scots Greys . . . . after receiving a loyal address by Provost Lawson, the procession was formed and the *cortège* proceeded slowly along Castle Street, by High Street, Nethergate, and South Tay Street, amongst every demonstration of loyalty and respect. On arriving at Dudhope Church, the public bodies drew aside, and the Royal party proceeded at a rapid pace. . . .'

Three weeks later Victoria returned to Dundee on her way home. Hundreds of Dundonians turned out to see the Queen and she recorded that 'on the pier the crush was very great.'

Victoria stopped again at Dundee in 1879 on her way from Balmoral. She noted: 'We reached the Tay Bridge station at six. Immense crowds everywhere, flags waving in every direction, and the whole population out; but one's heart was too sad for anything.' Victoria was mourning the death of Louis Napoleon, only child of Emperor Napoleon III and the Empress Eugénie. He had been killed a few days before in the Zulu War. Victoria noted: 'Janet Ely *(she was the Marchioness of Ely, Lady of the Bedchamber)* . . . showed us a Dundee paper, called the *Evening Telegraph*, which contained the fullest and most dreadful accounts. Monstrous!'

The Queen had more to say on the 1879 stop at Dundee: 'The Provost splendidly attired, presented an address. Ladies presented beautiful bouquets to Beatrice *(Princess Beatrice, Victoria's youngest daughter and companion)* and me . . .

'We stopped here about five minutes, and then began going over the marvellous Tay Bridge, which is rather more than a mile and a half long. It was begun in 1871. There were great difficulties in laying the foundation, and some lives were lost. It was finished in 1878.

'Mr Bouch, who was presented at Dundee, was the engineer. It took us, I should say, about eight minutes going over. The view was very fine.

'The boys of the training-ship *(Mars)*, with their band, looked very well . . .'

Victoria's mention of the *Evening Telegraph* (first published in March 1877) underlines the fact that her subjects in Dundee were very well-informed. By the beginning of her reign *The Dundee Advertiser* (first issued January 16th, 1801) was well established and was under the editorship of Sir John Leng from 1852 to 1906. The *Advertiser* emerged as a powerful voice in local and national politics. In 1861 it became a daily newspaper and ran alongside, and in competition with, the *Dundee Courier* (first issued September 20th, 1816). The *Courier* was amalgamated with the *Daily Argus* in 1861, and was firmly under the management of D.C. Thompson & Co Ltd from 1905.

It is from back numbers of papers such as these, which printed as much national as local news, that we can piece together the *ambiance* of Victorian Dundee and the part it played in Scottish social history. The chief industry of Dundee consisted of the manufacture of jute and heavy linen fabrics such as sailcloth; yet, the trade guides of the day give hundreds of addresses from those of shipbuilders, tea merchants, millers and dyers, to iron founders, engineers, cabinetmakers and watchmakers.

2.  H.M. Queen Victoria, born on May 24th, 1819 at Kensington Palace, reigned longer than any other British monarch. While she was on the throne, 1837-1901, Britain became the most powerful industrial nation in the world and the centre of the greatest Empire ever known.

3.  Albert Edward, Prince of Wales, photographed around his twenty-first birthday in 1862. As Edward VII he was renowned as a sportsman, *bon viveur* and lover of beautiful women.

One characterful trade was Victorian drapery which left its mark on Dundee shopfronts. As the Industrial Revolution developed, new customers had to be attracted, and one way of achieving this was to fit larger display windows to exhibit even grander and more attractive mountains of goods. The Dundee drapers sold all kinds of cloth, haberdashery and clothes. Inside the average Dundee draper's shop, like those of Draffen & Jarvie Ltd (1889), Henderson & Mackay (1858) and D.M. Brown's (1888), were highly polished counters with glass display cabinets and behind the counters, shelves and drawers reaching the ceiling. Assistants depended on commission from sales, as their pay was meagre: They would have had to have saved hard for weeks to afford a cotton shirt at 3/6 (17½p). The younger staff had the most miserable time, their hours were long; from 6am to midnight was not unknown. H.G. Wells, in his famous novel *The History of Mr Polly* (1910) struck much fellow-feeling among Dundonian shop assistants by his grim picture of shop life.

Drapery shops, in particular, provided 'making-up' services to customers. The orders for suits and dresses were fulfilled in workshops at the rear, or in nearby tenement rooms, where tailors, needlewomen and milliners worked. Those were the days of 'The Sweated Trades', a serious social evil all over industrial Britain. Workers in these trades (and not just drapery) did not enjoy the protection of the successive Factory Acts. Usually those involved in 'sweated labour' (hard work for little pay, in insanitary working conditions) were the women of the impoverished inner-city areas. The Anti-Sweated Labour League was formed in the 1880s to protect these unfortunates, but it was not until 1909, when the Trades Boards Act was passed—largely due to the efforts of Dundee MP Winston Churchill—that the disgraceful system was squeezed into oblivion.

The development of Dundee was a characteristic Victorian achievement, impressive in scale but limited in its vision. New opportunities were created as the city spread, but they also posed massive new problems. The people were undoubtedly better housed than they had been a hundred years earlier. Eighteenth century slums may have been pulled down, however without much care being given to the rehousing of slum dwellers.

An interesting insight into the living conditions of the time is to be seen in the *Report on Housing and Industrial Conditions in Dundee,* issued in 1905 by the Dundee Social Union. In its pages is a reflection of Victorian and Edwardian overcrowding with concomitant hardship. Most Dundonians of the period lived in one- or two-roomed houses. Rents remained fairly stable at 6d (2½p) at the beginning of Victoria's reign to 2/6 to 3/6 (12½p to 17½p) for a two-roomed dwelling. Yet, even by 1904 almost half of Dundee's population lived in overcrowded accommodation (24 percent of the houses had more than two persons per room). The rapidity of erection, the cheapness and poorness of materials for buildings led to houses being called 'jerry-built' (the word 'jerry' probably being derived from Jeremiah, the prophet of Gloom).

The Artisans Dwelling Act of 1875 gave the Dundee Council power to condemn and demolish insanitary housing, and the Housing of the Working Classes Act of 1890 gave the Council power to build houses. The evolution of the Water Closet was undoubtedly a Victorian phenomenon and an important part of social history. Dundee plumbers were to experience a 'boom' in sanitary trade following the *Report on the Sanitary Condition of the Labouring Population* (1842) by Sir Edwin Chadwick. Slowly, in the middle class habitations at first, the flush-out WC appeared in Dundee; many local ironmongers acted as agents for the unfortunately named WC manufacturer Thomas Crapper. George Stephen & Son (1814) and J & J Fleming (1841) were in the forefront of Dundee plumbing innovations. At least 1000 houses in Dundee had sanitary accommodation shared by +25 people, the norm being arrangements shared by 12 persons. By the early years of Victoria's reign the population of Dundee was 54,628, to rise in 1910 to 165,002.

Under the Scottish Bill for Parliamentary Reform of July 1832, Dundee received one MP, George S. Kinloch winning the seat for the Liberals. Parliamentary Reformers had fought hard in Dundee for their own representation since 1819; formerly, Dundee had been grouped with the burghs of Forfar, Perth, Cupar and St Andrews, and had rioted for its political independence. When Victoria came to the throne, Dundee was represented by Sir Henry Parnell.

The Liberals held sway in Dundee during the whole of Victoria and Edward's reigns. After 1868 there were two seats in Dundee, again held by the Liberals. In fact the constituency was rarely fought by the Conservatives (twice in over 50 years) with Liberals fighting Liberals. By 1887 two Home Rule Liberals (supporting self-government for Ireland) had beaten two Liberal Unionists (basically anti-Home Rule) for power. In the new parliament of 1906, Alexander Wilkie won a seat in Dundee for Labour, and in 1908 was joined by (the then Liberal) Rt. Hon. Winston Leonard Spencer Churchill to represent the city. In the year Edward VII died, Churchill was Home Secretary.

Politically Scotland remained consistent during Victoria's reign in its Radicalism, which was reflected in Dundee by the city's electoral devotion to the Liberals. This was due in no small measure to W.E. Gladstone, whose approach to the great problems of the day made a special appeal to Dundonians. Stern in principle, with a sense of moral right (rather than force), Gladstonian Liberalism purported to understand 'the will of the people'. The Nonconformist religious tone of Gladstonian utterances appealed to the granite-grey Calvinists of Dundee who had expunged the colourful symbols of Christianity from their Kirks. In Dundee the Church of Scotland retained a greater hold over the citizens than did the churches of the

4.    Like most British cities, Dundee ordered a statue of Queen Victoria cast in bronze to mark her Diamond Jubilee in 1897. It was unveiled outside the Albert Institute on Saturday August 26th, 1899 by her son H.R.H. Prince Arthur, Duke of Connaught (1850-1942), on a visit to Dundee in which he also opened the Victoria Hospital. The four bas reliefs on the sides of the statue depict: the marriage of Victoria and Prince Albert of Saxe-Coburg-Gotha, 1840; the Royal Visit to Dundee, 1844: the decoration of veterans of the Crimean War, 1854-56; and Her Majesty's sympathy with the poor.

English. In the city the ministers of such kirks as St Mary's were the custodians of the public conscience and were interpreters of theology, parish guardians, social welfare officers, burial board governors and educationalists all in one. As social welfare was predominantly a matter of charity during 1837-1910, the ministers were vital linkmen between those who had much to give and the needy. Such Dundee bequests as 'Thomas Smith Thomson's Bequest' (1862) of 6s (30p) monthly to the support of old men above 60 years of age was administered by the kirk. Old age pensions were not introduced until January 1st, 1909, at 5s (25p) per week for those over 70 years of age.

The gulf between rich and poor was ever emphasised from the pulpit. Yet, in Dundee's Howff Burial Ground there is engraved in stone above Agnes and Wellimina Robertson the well-loved Victorian comment:

> This World is like a city full of crooked streets,
> And Death the market place where all men meet;
> If life were merchandise to buy,
> The rich would live, and none but the poor would die.

The poor did die, in greater numbers than the rich in Dundee, as the epitaphs underline.

By and large political thought in Dundee was aimed at national and not local problems, as politics were dovetailed to national policy on such items as health, food and wages. During the mid-years of Victoria's reign, steps had been taken to make Dundee a healthier place. The Vaccination (Scotland) Act of 1863, making the vaccination of infants against smallpox

13

compulsory, led to a marked decline in the city of the disease. Other health matters were put in hand too, by the Public Health (Scotland) Act of 1897. One of the Victorian aspects of Dundee which was evident to any rural visitor in particular was the smoke nuisance. From time to time a pall of noisome smoke shrouded the city and the buildings took on a black aspect.

A study of the weekly wages in the Dundee jute mills gives a useful average scale of the domestic finances of the citizens. In 1905 skilled mechanics were earning 30s (£1.50) per week, with calendar workers at 19s (95p). A joiner might earn 34s (£1.70) and a plasterer 37s (£1.85), but many had a standard weekly wage of under £1. In real terms the average worker was little better off in 1910 than his grandfather had been in 1837.

In their study, the Dundee Social Union devoted a section to food. The daily menu of the average worker would be breakfast of porridge and milk, or bread and tea. Dinner ('lunch' was a middle class repast) might consist of broth made from ½lb of boiling beef (at 4½d, or 2p) with a pennyworth of vegetables and a halfpenny worth of barley. Rice was the most common pudding, with a 'clootie-dumpling' (usually boiled on the kitchen range in the pan with the soup!) for special occasions. The evening meal was no more than bread and butter for some, with maybe fish or ham for the workers of the family. Bread was the most expensive single item of the average diet, because so much was eaten; a 2lb loaf in 1904 cost 3d (1p).

Despite the Church of Scotland's aversion to alcohol and the kirk's official line that drunkenness was 'the principal moral cause of poverty' (report to the Royal Commission on the Poor Law and the Relief of Distress, 1910), there is no question that drunkenness was rife in Victorian and Edwardian Dundee. Dundee, in fact, was low on the list of convictions for drunkenness. Mild beer cost around 1½d (4p) per pint, with whisky at 3s (or 15p) per 24 fl oz bottle, or 2p (1p) per nip—methylated spirits worked out a 3d (1p) per bottle!

When Victoria came to the throne there were still two Scotlands, divided in the age-old way North-South into Highlands and Lowlands. The Scottish realm which she handed over to her son was now divided between East and West; largely due to the industrialisation and the Hibernisation of Clydeside. Dundee, however, was well on its way to being 'Anglicised'. The upper strata of Dundee society were increasingly being educated in English schools and universities, and its commerce was steadily coming under the control of English capitalism.

Albert Edward, Prince of Wales, was born at Buckingham Palace at forty-eight minutes past ten on the morning of Tuesday, November 9th, 1841, five years before Sir James Young Simpson began using chloroform in childbirth. It was not the last time either that Edward was to give his mother pain. Edward, who unwillingly underwent a cruel and unremitting education intended to produce 'the most perfect man' (that was his mother's definition of Albert, the Prince Consort), was always 'difficult'. He was far too like her womanising 'wicked uncles' (the sons of George III) for Victoria's liking and she never wholly trusted him, denying him access to the administration of her realm. Consequently, Edward VII knew little, in real terms, of his new kingdom, and less of Scotland, except its contribution to his vast appetite and sporting pleasures.

Portly and fun-loving, Edward VII was sixty years old when he became king following his mother's death at Osborne House, Isle of Wight, in January 1901. Although he passed through Dundee on his way to Royal Deeside, the new king never made an official visit to Dundee. Indeed, it is likely that his knowledge of the city was summed up in the old cliché, 'Jute and Marmalade': James Keiller & Son Ltd, the inventors of 'Dundee Marmalade', had been established in 1797.

The age of Edward VII, was a period of affluence and ostentation, of strict social discipline, of peace and plenty. It was an age too, of unrest and poverty, of uncertainty about Britain's place in the world, as well as of growing concern that so very much was owned by so few. This

14

short but intensely active period 1901-1910 was, in total, a time of transition between the leisurely self-confident Victorian age, and the bursting revolutionary years which were to be heralded by the event of World War I.

The industrial explosion of the Victorian era wrenched a large part of the rural society, that had predominated in Angus, away from the dominating traditions of the landed aristocracy. Politics too had been manipulated by men who, for the most part, derived their position from the fact that they owned property: Now a new social force was at work. Part of the nation's wealth was now earned in Dundee, and the men who practised it therein were beginning to exert their influence in government and other fields.

It was this economic necessity that forced the majority of Edward's subjects to move from rural areas to cities like Dundee. The importation of cheap food from America and the Colonies made it impossible to grow food economically in Britain, with the result that the flow of agricultural workers into Dundee increased. So Edwardian Dundee was bustling and bursting at the seams.

The standard of living of Dundee's increasing well-to-do was dependent on a low rate of income tax (1s, or 5p in the £ on income above £160 per annum) and on the plentiful supply of domestic servants. 'Service' was an increasing field of employment for women in Edwardian Dundee. A 'tweenie' in a 'big hoose' might earn £12 a year, with ambitions of the dizzy heights of housekeeper at £80 per year; while a boy, on £10 a year as a hallboy, might advance eventually to the £100 per year of a butler.

Through the Education (Scotland) Act of 1872, the state for the first time accepted directly the responsibility of educating children. Even so, the unit of administration remained the parish, burgh or city, and in the case of Dundee, ratepayers were enjoined to elect a school board of between five and fifteen members. The immediate task was to build extra schools and to enforce attendance as far as possible. The Act further required school boards to appoint teachers, pay their salaries and levy a local rate for education, and fix the amount of school fees that children's should pay. At first the charge was around 3d (1p) per week, but after the Act of 1890, elementary education became virtually 'free' in Dundee.

The era spawned a number of Dundee schools of interest to educational historians. One such was the New Industrial School for Girls, which was opened by Lady Ogilvie Dalgleish on Wednesday, June 24th 1896. The school was founded by the Industrial Schools Society (1846) 'for the purpose of checking the increase of juvenile crime in the city'. Another landmark in education came with the Education (Scotland) Act of 1908, which provided for medical examinations in schools and made schooling compulsory for children between five and fourteen, with an expanding of advanced education beyond fourteen.

Around 1870, too, evolved what was called 'the Dundee Movement', a grassroots feeling that developed towards establishing a university in Dundee. Between 1870 and 1875 courses of lectures for adults were established, in various literary and scientific subjects, in Dundee and neighbouring areas, as the Victorian thirst for knowledge grew. In 1883 University College was opened in Dundee mainly through the public-spirited actions of the Baxter family of Balgavies.

With the development of education, the Edwardian Age was hailed by some as the 'Children's Age'. Undoubtedly the Edwardians did make great advances in providing for the care and instruction of children, but the century did not develop as the Edwardians had hoped; of this they had almost immediate evidence—children who first partook of nursery education (the first Scottish nursery school was opened in the Canongate, Edinburgh, in 1906), for instance, were old enough to fight in World War I. 'Protection' of children was given much impetus in Edwardian Dundee. Under the provision of the Children Act of 1909, no child was allowed into a bar where alcoholic drinks were being consumed. The Café Royal, in High Street and Thorter Row, had a 'children's dining room' where children could be isolated from the wine and spirit consuming diners elsewhere. Temperance volunteers, who met in Lamb's Temperence Hotel (Reform St), would station themselves outside the Dundee public houses to look after the children while their elders were becoming 'legless' inside!

Social welfare of Victorian and Edwardian times was very much a matter of private charity. The Dundee Institute for the Blind was such a fund. Founded in 1865, mainly by the Molisons of Errol Park, the Institute moved to Magdalen Green in 1884. A brochure of the day noted the Institute's intent: 'The work of the Institute may be divided into three departments—(1). A school for the education, both general and industrial, of children up to the age of 16. (2). A Musical School for training, for the musical profession, blind persons above school age; the education given including not only musical but general subjects, so as to fit the students for the position in life to which their profession entitles them. (3). An Industrial Department in which persons above the age of 16 are instructed in various trades and industries, and in which these are carried on by other blind employees. The trades and industries engaged in include Basket, Brush, Mat, and Mattress making and Upholstery. Firelighter-making, Feather and Hair Cleaning and Wood chopping and bundling. In addition to the premises at Magdalen Green, the Institution has a Sale Shop at 30 High St, Dundee.

'The number of persons receiving benefit from the Institution at the close of the last financial year (1900) was 101. The amount of goods sold by the Institution during the year was £8,553 5s 4d, and the wages paid to the blind workers amounted to £2,065 10s 10d.' This worked out at around 7s 10d (£0.39) per week!

In Victorian and Edwardian Dundee entertainment and leisure was very much by social class, and was governed by mobility. Up to the 1860s tourism and holidays were only for the wealthy; in fact, when Victoria's reign commenced there was no holiday at Christmas for either rich or poor. Christmas, to a large extent, was the creation of the Prince Consort and Charles Dickens, Prince Albert popularised the Christmas Tree and Dickens's book *A Christmas Carol* was published in 1843. A great stimulus was given to holiday-making in 1871 by the Act which established Bank Holidays. Dundee people of all classes now started to take holidays by the sea, and the train made day trips to scenic spots a vogue.

Strolling and walking too, became a popular pastime. The fashionable paraded in their finery both morning and afternoon, but the working class generally took the air on Sunday afternoons (many having redeemed their best clothes from a pawn shop for the day). Parks were used by all classes and became a Victorian city phenomenon. 'The Arbroath Road is a favourable walk with Dundonians,' commented a Victorian guide book of Dundee. 'On Sunday evenings it is crowded by young and old, anxious to inhale the air that comes from both land and sea.' Most were making for Baxter Park, donated by Sir David Baxter and his sisters, and laid out to a design by Sir Joseph Paxton, the architect of the Crystal Palace; others preferred the Victorian 'hobby' of cemetery strolling and epitaph reading and were making for the city's Eastern Necropolis hailed as 'Dundee's finest cemetery' which had been opened in 1862.

Partaking of lunch (2.00pm was the most usual hour) and afternoon tea outside the home was popularised in Victorian times. Consequently tea rooms blossomed in Dundee. One of the first was in D.M. Brown's (established 1888) in the High Street: Brown's publicity department had this to say of their facilities: 'Tea rooms, as an adjunct to the Drapers' Business, occurred first to the inventive Parisian. The Bright American quickly followed, and the Londoner came in a good third. Since then the Tea and Luncheon Rooms in the larger Department Establishments throughout the country have become an accepted feature. The first in Dundee is D.M. Brown's. The Tea and Luncheon Room proper is large and airy. It is clean. Its appearance is handsome and the decorations in good taste. There is a ladies' Writing and Reading Room, Cloak Room and Toilet Rooms. There is a Gentleman's Office in which every convenience will be found for gentlemen meeting to transact business. Everything plain or dainty is supplied at moderate prices. The Service is quick, and of the pleasantest description. No charge is made for any service rendered, and gratuities are not accepted.'

After being refreshed in such establishments the middle class Dundonian might retire to the 1700-seat Her Majesty's Theatre and Opera House (opened October 19th, 1885) to see a comic opera, a concert, or a musical. Mostly the working classes, while patronising a music hall (the Livermore Brothers opened the People's Palace in Lochee Road in 1891), or a circus, from time to time, preferred sport as a leisure activity, from roller-skating to dancing, and from curling to boxing, cycle racing and athletics. The development of Edwardian delight in leisure activities outdoors led to such inventions as the Thermos flask, expensive at 21/6 (£1.07½p) for the pint size.

In Victoria's day Broughty Ferry had developed as a pleasant seaside suburb of Dundee. Writing in 1894, William Kidd (1835-1916), the famous author-printer of the *Guide to Dundee,* wrote of Broughty Ferry: 'The Ferry is a favourite place of residence of the merchant princes of Dundee, whose palatial mansions occupy every point of vantage on the rising ground to north and east. Of late years, great improvements have been affected to the class of houses erected in the lower part of the village, and elegant shops have sprung up to supply the population with all the necessities and elegancies which a well-to-do population demand'.

By the 1890s, of course, Broughty Ferry had become the third largest town in Angus. The town had been formed into a Burgh in 1863 under the General Police and Improvement (Scotland) Act of 1862. In 1901 a Town Council was formed for Broughty Ferry under the Town Council (Scotland) Act of 1900; but, the town had had provosts since 1892. The first being Provost James Guthrie Orchar, whose name is immortalised in Orchar Park and the Orchar Gallery on the Esplanade which is still run by private trust.

The development of Broughty Ferry was remarkable, for, in the early 1800s, the area was no more than a cluster of fisherman's houses set near the foreshore and dominated by its then ruined 15th century castle. In 1841 the castle had become a coastguard station, but was soon to become a storage depot for the Edinburgh and Northern Railway Co. Indeed it was the railway transporting summer visitors for sea bathing which had really helped to change Broughty Ferry from a white fish and herring hamlet into a modern town. Most visitors came from Dundee itself on the Caledonian Railway's return 'bathers'' ticket of 6d (2½p). Purchased in 1855, Broughty Ferry castle was re-equipped—and re-built in its present form— as a fortress and gun battery by the War Office in 1860. From 1860 to 1908 the castle was garrisoned by Coastal Defence Volunteers, Artillery and Submarine Miners; from 1908 onwards it was used by units of the Territorial Army. Broughty Ferry was not officially annexed to Dundee until 1913.

Broughty Ferry castle and the Angus and Fife shores of the Tay were popular scenes for the Victorian and Edwardian painter and photographer. Dundee scenes were amongst the earliest Scottish photographs. Some two years after Queen Victoria came to the throne, practical methods of photography were announced. Although a French invention—Joseph Nicéphore Niepce (1765-1832) took what is generally considered to be the first photograph— photography was first popularised in an amateur way in Scotland. With the active support of the scientist Sir David Brewster (1781-1868), Principal of the United Colleges, St Andrews University, the inventor William Henry Fox Talbot (1800-77) sought to develop his original photographic research.

Fox Talbot developed in 1840 a way to record likenesses—the calotype. He patented his invention in 1841 as a 'talbotype', and was anxious that his system be popularised. Fox

Talbot wished for recognition which had been given to the Frenchman Louis Jacques Mandé Daguerre (1789-1851), whose pictures on an iodised plate *(daguerréotypes)* had won him international fame. Scotland was not hampered by the strict restrictions on copyright as England, so Fox Talbot wanted to corner the market. With the help of Brewster and others, like Dr John Adamson (1809-70), of St. Andrews, Fox Talbot's invention was secured and launched as an art form.

From 1843 to around 1878 photography was very much the work of academic dabblers. It was too expensive a process for the general Dundee hobbyist. There were, of course, 'itinerant photographers' who came to the city, took rooms in a hotel and advertised in the papers for local custom. Their photographs were mostly vapid poses and generally this was a summer occupation. Yet the development of photography in Scotland caught the imagination of many in Dundee spurred on by the famous landscape painter David Octavius Hill (1802-70) and the distinguished commercial photographer Thomas Annan.

Following the inventions of such as Richard Leach Maddox, by the later 1870s the amateur could buy photographic material without employing the tedious, skilled process of making each chemical. In 1888 George Eastman of New York patented the first box camera. This transformed the practice of photography and thousands of ordinary folk were able to develop the pastime. As the camera and photographic shop was a development following World War II, it was the Dundee chemists who stocked photographic materials. Such chemists as Johnston & Adams (1875) and J.W. Robertson (1895) became prominent photographic dealers in Dundee.

An enormous boost to commercial photography came with the popularity of the picture postcard, many dealers adding the words 'a real photograph' to their wares. Head and shoulders above all others, of course, was Messrs Valentine of Dundee who were established as greeting card manufacturers in 1825. By the time Edward came to the throne, the picture postcard was an accepted part of Dundee life, and had its 'Golden Age' 1902-18.

Edward VII's reign ended on May 6th 1910, when the king died at Buckingham Palace. Dundonians now slipped with the nation into a depressing era which was to end in the most costly conflict that the world has ever known in 1914. Thousands who had been Victorians and Edwardians were slaughtered on the fields of Flanders, and those who were left were to experience industrial and civil discontent which came to a climax in the General Strike of 1926.

In this book are photographs which help to paint a picture of the social changes which took place in Dundee and Broughty Ferry 1837 to 1910. It is a collection of characteristics and moods which could only have been captured by the camera, which in Victoria's day first became an indispensable recorder of everyday history.

RAYMOND LAMONT-BROWN

CHAPTER ONE

# TRADES PROFESSIONS AND CRAFTS

TO dismiss employment in Victorian and Edwardian Dundee as no more than 'Jute and Whaling' is to rob the city of its rich commercial heritage. Engineering, railways, ships, department stores, factories of many kinds all contributed to Dundee's major categories of employment. Yet, a look through any collection of Victorian and Edwardian 'work' photographs identifies two areas of particular interest. The large numbers of women employed, and the ubiquitousness of itinerants and small traders who have vanished from modern street scenes.

In the early years of Victoria's reign, from 1841 to 1847, factory legislation was centred upon the employment of women. Many feared that women might displace men operatives altogether in Dundee factories. This fear was lessened by the passing of the Ten Hours Bill (1848) restricting women and children to a ten hour day. In the less well regulated and predominantly workshop trades in Dundee, it was still possible to work a 12 hour day, even up to 1900. The average in Dundee was 60 hours per week (say, in the 1870s). By 1870 no child could work under the age of 8; from 8-13 a maximum working day was prescribed as 6½ hours as well as at least 10 hours a week compulsory education.

In Dundee large numbers of people scraped a living in the streets as bootblacks, match-sellers, ice-cream vendors, knife-grinders, baked potato and lemonade sellers. The photographs herein show them with their air of shabby respectability, but demanding hard work.

Dundee was in the forefront of trade unionism with workers seeking democratic ideals in exchange for industrious behaviour. As Edward's reign developed these ideals gave way to a single objective of solidarity.

By the end of Edward's reign Dundee's employees had raised themselves from being no more than beasts of burden whose existence Victoria's first Prime Minister, Lord Melbourne, had treated with indifference, to having at least the dignity of ordinary human beings. By comparison the state of Dundee's employers and professional men, had changed little. They had not had to endure the poverty or foul working conditions or the uncertainties of employment. Legislation and enlightenment contributed throughout Victoria's reign to the gradual improvement of working conditions. The musty austerity of work places like Ebenezer Scrooge's counting house, gave way to offices better planned and considerably more cheerful. Yet one thing the Victorian and Edwardian camera does show is the lamentable demise of the self-employed craftsman whose pride of trade and artistry was so much a part of their contemporary society.

The photography shows how the pace of life was very much slower in Victorian and Edwardian Dundee and the pursuit of material wealth was substantially less than it is today. The city had a bustle about it that had charm. Each shop had its staff of delivery boys and many establishments remained open until about eight in the evening. Daily the road to Broughty Ferry teemed with the deliveries of goods to the well-to-do whose houses were run by a plethora of servants all proud of their place in the city's workforce.

19

5.    Mechanisation in the shipbuilding industry and the dockland areas was slow and primitive for much of the Victorian Era. Teams of men were always needed. The big clipper ships brought men of many nationalities to work on Dundee's waterfront.

6.

Coal being carted from the docks. Unusually for a city so close to the coalfields of Fife much of Dundee's coal came from Northumberland. Coal merchants in Dundee delivered their coal in measures known as metts, and half-metts, which were peculiar to Dundee. A half-mett weighed 84lbs and was said to be a more convenient weight for carrying up the 3 floors of a tenement than the traditional hundredweight.

7.    Street traders display their wares by the Royal Arch. This was probably the overspill from the Greenmarket, and contained collections of household items from dispossessions.

8.    Delivery van of the wholesale confectioners Messrs T.B. Kidd. Like every large city, Victorian and Edwardian Dundee had many small retail and wholesale grocers. At the turn of the century there were somewhere in the region of 100 grocers in Dundee's west end alone.

9.    'Charming Birds for the small sum of one penny,' reads the caption on the cage belonging to this Italian organ grinder. Once, these itinerant 'musicians' were a common sight in upper working class and middle class Dundee streets.

10.   Traction engine about 1900. Such engines were a necessary form of power on farm and in factory yard from the 1880s.

11. Ice cream cart outside the Albert Institute around 1900. There was a good sized Italian Community in Dundee which arrived from the 1880s onwards. Most made their living selling such foods as fish and chips, confectionery and, in summer, ice cream. The ice cream sellers pushed their brightly painted vans through the streets selling no cones, nor fancy things, just penny 'sliders' slapped up with a pair of wooden patters. The statue of Burns was erected in 1880 and is a bronze replica of Sir John Steele's statue in New York. Burns is shown meditating on his lost 'Highland Mary in Heaven'. The cost of the statue was 1000 guineas and the pedestal £230, the money being raised by means of a Bazaar.

12.    The clerical staff of J & A.D. Grimond's jute works, taken 30th March 1907.

| John S Ramsay | Carpet Order Clerk | Head Office | G Patterson | Clerk | Mill Office |
|---|---|---|---|---|---|
| John Rodgers | Apprentice Clerk | Mill | J H Macfarland | Cashier | Head Office |
| J Johnson | Apprentice Clerk | Mill | A A Taylor | Clerk | Hessian Dept |
| A Melville | Apprentice Clerk | Mill | John Goodfellow | App Clerk | Maxwelltown Works |
| John S Watson | Clerk | Head Office | Wm Smith | Clerk | B B Calendar |
| Robt. Smith | Book keeper | Head Office | Jas Guthrie | Clerk | B B Calendar |
| John McQueen | Clerk | P.L. Factory | Alex Miles | Clerk | B B Calendar |
| Robt. Mains | Clerk | Head Office | Miss A M Dewar | Typist | Head Office |
| Ken D White | Clerk | Head Office | Miss J E Stowell | Typist | Head Office |
| Alex C Campbell | Yarn Order clerk | Head Office | Miss A L Coyle | Typist | Head Office |
| Will C Gow | Twine salesman | Head Office | David Fraser | Clerk | Maxwelltown Works |
| Will G Fair | Yarn salesman | Head Office | Lindsay Keith | Clerk | Head Office |
| A S McKenzie | Hessian salesman | Head Office | Wm Laird | Clerk | Maxwelltown Works |
| Wm Swann | Sec and Treasurer | | Chas Kelly | Designer | Maxwelltown Works |
| L G Macintyre | Joint Managing Director | | A O Thompson | Clerk | Mill Office |
| Wm Strange | Telephone Exchange | Head Office | John Phin | Clerk | Mill Office |
| Geo Kirk | Engineer | B.B. Works | David Robertson | Clerk | Mill Office |
| Andrew Reid | Clerk | P.L. Factory | Robt Taylor | Clerk | Mill Office |
| Mr Charles Pearson | Manager | B B Works | J S R Smith | App Clerk | Mill Office |
| John White | Manager | B B Works | Wm Cowper | Clerk | Mill Office |
| E G Gib | Manager | Maxwelltown Works | H Laird | Manager | Head Office |
| W C Smith | Spinning Manager | B B Works | J C Crammond | App Clerk | B B Calendar |
| Robt Reid | Factory Manager | B B Works | Geo Mooney | Office Boy | Mill Office |
| James Wallace | Clerk | B B Calendar | F F Robertson | App Clerk | Head Office |
| C.W. Crosby | Designer | Maxwelltown Works | David Brown | App Clerk | Head Office |
| Robt Grieve | Shipping Clerk | Maxwelltown Works | W Chalmers | App Clerk | Mill Office |
| Jas Anderson | Carpet Salesman | Head Office | H F Slidders | Twine Order Clerk | Head Office |
| J S Kerr | Cashier | Mill Office | | | |

13. Trade Union Officials, Dundee Branch of the Painters Society, 1909.
*Top row:* Jas. Donaldson (Chairman); Wm. Davie (Committee); Geo. Robertson (Trustee); H. Duncan (Committee).
*Middle row:* P. Brodie (Committee); Ed. McGill (Trustee); Jas. McKenzie (Committee); Jas. Brysun (Trustee); Jas.
Townsend (Committee). *Front row:* D. Milne (Committee); M. Hughes (Committee); T. England (Sec); J. Pugh
(President); R. Bowman (Treasurer); M. Quinn (Auditor). The banner reads: 'Art makes the man, not man the Art', a
paraphrase of a line from *Essay XV* of Hume's *The Epicurean*.

14. Porters, Dundee Docks, circa 1900.

15. Itinerant tradesmen were a feature of Victorian and
Edwardian Dundee. This one, a furniture mender,
specifies cane chairs as his speciality.

16.    Stall holders selling fruit and patent medicines by the Royal Arch. The large crowd in the background may be gathered to send off one of the whaling fleets. 'Rowlands Paregoric' was a form of analgesic and like all patent medicines was a compound of balsam and faith.

# JUTE AND TEXTILES IN DUNDEE

FROM the 1500s Dundee has been associated with the textile industry. Wool, linen, hemp and plaiding were originally the mainstay of Dundee trade and were instrumental in developing links between Dundee and the Baltic.

Jute—fibre from the bark of the plants *Corchorus capsularis* and *C. olitorius,* imported chiefly from Bengal, and used for cordage, canvas and so on—made Dundee internationally famous. Following the discovery by William Taylor, at Ruthven Mill, that jute could be softened by the addition of whale oil, this led to the successful spinning of jute. So by 1839 the jute industry had taken a firm hold in Dundee, because of the landing of whale oil in the city. The business was further developed by the use of jute for coffee bagging by the East Indies traders. The first complete shipload of around 300 tons of jute was landed in Dundee in 1840; by 1866 the loads had reached 62,000 tons a year to reach 277,000 tons in 1895. This 'golden age of jute' was boosted by three wars—the Crimean War 1854-56, the American Civil War 1860-61, and the Franco-Prussian War of 1870—for hostilities stopped the availability of flax and jute was substituted.

Some main manufacturers of this period were: J & A.D. Grimond Ltd (est 1835); Bell & Balfour (est 1780); Cox Brothers Ltd (est 1700); Gilroy, Sons & Co Ltd (est 1848), they were amongst the first Dundee manufacturers to establish a direct importation of jute from India.

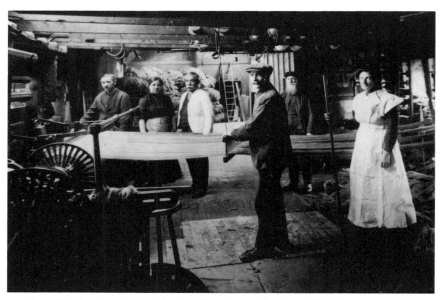

17.     The dry-beaming machine in a Dundee weaving-shop, Hillside works, 1911.
        Piles of hand wound link chains are placed to one side.

18. Weavers, Mid-Wynd works, circa 1850.

19. Rolling, measuring and calendaring machines, and the men who worked them, all crushed into one workshop. Nelson Street Works, 1911.

20.    Dundee looms from the Blackness Foundry at Hillside Works, 1911.

21. Polepark Jute Works decorated for the marriage of one of the Smith family (owners), circa 1900.

22. Polepark Jute works, circa 1898.

23.    Dock workers unloading jute bales on board a jute ship, 1910.

# THE MILITARY MEN

THE Victorian vision of peace and plenty was rudely disrupted in 1854 by the outbreak of the Crimean War. With its causes lost in a jumble of religious, economic and nationalistic motives, the Crimean War gave the ordinary people of Britain newspaper tales of guts and heroism. Alma, Inkerman and Balaclava were far-away battles on which every Dundee urchin was an expert, little realising the incompetence therein of the British War Office and the callous ineptitude of the Government, led by Lord Aberdeen. Yet, after this war the sight of a 'military man' in the street sent a swelling of pride into the bosom of every Dundonian. In reality the Crimean War was a savage rebuff to Victorian pride and self-confidence—albeit a boost to Dundee commerce—and the lessons of the conflict were dearly bought. Sixty years on, Victoria's grandsons Kaiser Wilhelm II and George V were to discover that those lessons had been largely forgotten.

Following the French Revolution, 'sympathy rioting' took place in Dundee in 1792. Thereafter the government sub-leased Dudhope Castle as a military headquarters from the Douglas family, the titular Constables of Dundee. It remained a barracks until August 1880. The castle and grounds were bought by the city in 1893. The policies of the castle were long used as military parade grounds, and troops were stationed here during the two world wars; in 1914 Dudhope was occupied by officers of the 4th Battalion, The Black Watch.

24.   1st Forfarshire Artillery Volunteers. Repository drill showing the gun being mounted onto its carriage prior to field manoeuvres.

25.   Tay Division Royal Engineers (Volunteer) Submarine Miners, Annual Inspection, Broughty Ferry, 1899. The division was raised on 17th March 1888 and disbanded in 1908. A feature to notice is the pipe band. Royal Engineers did not normally possess pipe bands; but, the Tay Division did, being **Scottish**.

26.   Officers of the Dundee Highlanders (The Black Watch) Rifle Volunteers outside Dudhope Castle, 1885. The two officers (standing centre) are most probably the Colonel and his Adjutant. For horseback riding they wore top boots and had the handle of their basket hilted swords removed. The other officers wear full dress uniform consisting of Highland Doublet, tartan trews, plaid and spiked helmet.

27. Dudhope Castle built at the close of the sixteenth century was the fortress home of the Constable of Dundee. The last owner to live in the castle was Lord Douglas of Douglas; his successor, the Victorian 12th Earl of Home was the 27th and last Titular Constable. In the foreground of the castle a gun assembly class are ranged.

28. A prize-winning team of Artillery volunteers pose for the camera around 1898. The 32lb cannon is ready to be run onto its carriage. The anonymity of khaki was reserved for the field of battle, for those who 'served the Queen' there was the appeal of a smart uniform.

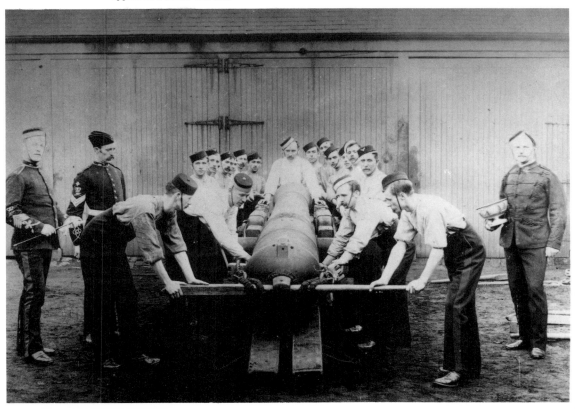

# WHALING

HERMAN Melville's *Moby Dick* (1851) and F.T. Bullen's *The Cruise of the Cachalot* (1906), were stirring whaling tales for youngsters in Victorian and Edwardian Dundee and Broughty Ferry. Yet, many a child along the shores of Tay had their own personal tales to recount as their fathers served aboard Dundee whalers.

Whales have been hunted since the 9th century with the Norwegians and the Basques as pioneers in the industry. Whaling and sealing, and their by-products, were important employment factors for Dundee folk. The work of the whalers was divided into two seasons. In the Spring, they hunted seals off Greenland or Newfoundland; and in Summer whaled in the Davis Straits, off Canada and Greenland. By the mid-years of Victoria's reign, the Dundee whaling fleet comprised 10 steam ships of 270-439 tons. The Dundee Whaling Co and the Tay Whale Fishing Co owned half of the ships between them. In 1872 Dundee was Britain's leading whaling port.

Consequently Dundee was in the forefront of whaling innovations. By 1875 steam engines were installed in the Dundee whaler *Tay,* which set the fashion in northern waters. In 1870, Foya, a Norwegian invented the shot-harpoon, which revolutionised whale fishing and made it more deadly, the harpoon being shot from a gun into a vital part of the sea monsters. 1878-80 were good years for the Dundee whalers but the trade declined in the 1890s fundamentally because of the use of mineral oil instead of whale oil in the jute industry. It cost around £5000 to £6000 per season per ship to run an outfit; so,4 whales and many seals were necessary per trip to make it profitable.

29.    The Dundee whaler *Eclipse* moored to an ice floe during a whaling voyage to the Davis Straits. *Eclipse* was not a Dundee built whaler but came to the city in 1892 from Peterhead. She had been built in 1867 by Alex Hall & Co, Aberdeen, for Captain D. Gray of Peterhead on 'the lines of the successful Dundee steamers'. Last records of her are as a Russian Survey vessel in 1936.

30. A walrus caught feeding her pup on the ice floe. Numbers of Walrus were often shot by whalers during a voyage as a source of blubber (oil), ivory (tusks) and for their hides. The female in the picture is likely to be dead, but the pup was still alive when the photograph was taken.

31. A polar bear with her two cubs on the deck of a Dundee whaler. Polar bears were shot for their skins whenever the opportunity arose.

32.    Flensing—cutting up to remove the blubber—a whale aboard a Dundee whaler.

33.
The Dundee steam whaler
*Active* in the icepack
during a voyage to the
Davis Straits. The *Active*
was one of the older
Dundee whalers sailing to
the Arctic from 1852 after
she was built in
Peterhead.

34.    William Norrie, fisherman, Broughty Ferry.        (overleaf)

35. Two old fisherfolk on the shore at Broughty Ferry.

36. Fishermen mending their nets while ashore; Broughty Ferry castle is in the background.

37.    Broughty Ferry fishermen 'barking' nets. 'Barking' was designed to preserve the nets against the corrosive effects of the sea water. The nets were boiled in vats of water and woodbark and taken to the fields behind the town to dry.

38.    One group of itinerant entertainers were the White Coons, who came to Broughty Ferry in the summer seasons. They performed their shows from a wooden stand on the beach. Circa 1899.

39.  Firebrigade, Polepark Juteworks. Jute was a highly inflammable fabric because of the whale oil used to soften it. Many jute works possessed their own firebrigades.

40.  Police Black Maria outside the Sheriff Courts, Bell Street, Dundee. Circa 1910. Driver D. McIntosh, and Constable J. Anderson are on the box. Constable J. Cruickshank stands at the rear. Note the differing police uniforms.

CHAPTER TWO

# SPIRES, ARCHES AND TOWERS

WE are liable to think of the Victorian way of building, and the Victorian home, in the same way as we consider the Victorians themselves—as essentially middle class, staid and industrious. Victorian and Edwardian Dundee, however, presents those interested in architecture with the whole gamut of building, from the stately town houses of the wealthy to the gut-rending poverty of the feckless and underprivileged.

So wide a prospect cannot be taken in a single glance, so the photographs in this section should be viewed more than once. First for the intrigue of the social history; then within the scheme of the book comparing them with the other examples in other chapters; and once again, to study the tastes of the Victorian and Edwardian builders working in Dundee and Broughty Ferry.

Helped by the photographs in this book we can look back to the beginning of Victoria's reign, when urban development was in its infancy, and the Regency influences which still abounded, then forward to the 1880s and 1890s when developments in science and art had transformed much of the architectural landscape and the domestic habitat. An interesting facet to note is how the styles of the earlier era were less genteel, and how they developed into the ostentatious and often tastlessness of Victorian public works, moving further to the inelegant styles of Edwardian public and private opulence.

It was an age of clutter and dirt, a world of gothic extravagance and bric-à-brac—but as in Samuel Smiles's dictum, Victorian buildings reflected 'A Place for Everything, and Everything in its Place'.

41. The second Royal Infirmary, built 1852-55, photographed shortly after its opening. Behind the cemetery (today the site of a carpark) the incline and pulley brackets of the winding engine of the Dundee-Newtyle railway can be seen. The winding engine was used to pull trains up and down the Law.

42. The original Royal Arch was erected in 1844 for the visit of Queen Victoria and Prince Albert. It was designed in wood as a temporary structure for the Royal couple to walk through after their landing. The Arch was replaced by a new one in stone in 1851, designed by J.T. Rochead, which stood until it was demolished to make way for the Tay Road Bridge in the early 1960s. Note the Midland Railway Carriage. Although English railways did not run services in this area, they often maintained delivery carts.

43. The Caledonian Railway Station, circa 1905. The Caledonian, or West Station, was built in 1899 on the site of a previous station. It was demolished in 1964 to make way for the approach to the Tay Road Bridge.

44. Trades Hall, circa 1875. Built in 1778 and demolished in 1878, the Trades Hall stood in front of the present Clydesdale Bank at the east end of the High Street. It was the meeting place of the Nine Incorporated Trades of Dundee: Bakers, Shoemakers, Glovers, Tailors, Bonnetmakers, Fleshers, Hammermen, Weavers and Dyers, who each had their own room in the building. The shield which shows the coats of arms of the nine trades, seen in the picture, is today preserved in St Mary's Tower.

45.    The Clydesdale Bank, around 1890. Opened in 1878 the bank was initially hidden behind the Trades Hall at the east end of the High Street. Its glorious facade was revealed after the demolition of the Trades Hall.

46. The Wishart Arch, Cowgate. The arch, part of the city walls, was built in the sixteenth century and named after the Protestant Martyr George Wishart, burnt at St Andrews in 1546. It is doubtful that Wishart himself preached from the site. The arch was repaired in the nineteenth century using old gravestones which can still be seen. Through the arch can be viewed the Wishart Church, where Mary Slessor (see Plates 106-107) worshipped, and the 'John o'Groats' pub on its ground floor. This unusual combination of church and pub gave the building its nickname of 'Heaven and Hell'.

47. The High School, 1910. The High School was built in the Meadows, an area of public common, in 1832 at a cost of some £10,000. It was designed by the architect George Angus and was originally known as the Public Seminaries.

48. The Royal Exchange, Panmure Street, built in 1853 by the architect David Bryce. It was modelled on the fifteenth century cloth halls of Flanders, and the tower was originally intended to be surmounted by an octagon and crown. The architect, however, reckoned without the boggy nature of the Meadows, which soon caused the foundations to crack, and the octagon project had to be abandoned.

49. Union Hall, circa 1874, was originally built by the Episcopalians as a place of worship, but received its name when it was used from 1851 by the Dundee Literary Societies Union. Note in the photograph the lower rooms which were rented out as commercial premises. The building stood on an island in the middle of the High Street, opposite the Trades Hall, blocking the entrance to the Nethergate and was regarded as an eyesore and inconvenience. Lawson's Guide to Dundee in 1870 claimed 'its removal would be universally hailed as a great public improvement.' It was demolished in August 1876 and was replaced by the Caird Fountain at the top of Whitehall Street in 1879.

50. Broughty Castle and Old Windmill, circa 1860. The old windmill, on the site of the present Castle Green, was used by the local joiner and woodturner in the mid-Victorian years. Broughty Castle can be seen in the distance before its restoration by the War Office in 1861.

51. **The Albert Institute.** Following the Public Libraries and Museum (Scotland) Act a number of prominent citizens of Dundee decided to build an Institute dedicated to Science, Literature and the Arts and Crafts. It was built in memory of Albert, the Prince Consort, and the commission was given to the famous 'Gothick' architect Sir Gilbert Scott, who built the main body of the Institute including the famous swirling staircase. The building opened as a reference library in 1869. It was extended in 1873 to house the museum, and again between 1887-89 by the architect William Alexander.

52.  The Old Customs House, circa 1872. Built in the sixteenth century and formerly the town house of Provost Pierson, the building originally had three turrets similar in design to those at Dudhope Castle. These were later truncated when they became unsafe. The building was used as a Customs House in the late eighteenth century, but when a new Customs House was built in 1843, at the entrance to the docks area, it **was used for retailing.**

53.  Cholera Hospital, Fish Street, circa 1875. This was originally a tenement building, but was taken over as a hospital during the cholera epidemic of 1832. It stood on the site of the Tay Centre (formerly Mather's Hotel), and was demolished in the 1880s.

54.  The sloping shops at Bonnethill, 1875. Lawson's butchers sold more pork and veal in this working class area, as this was cheaper than beef or mutton.

55.  Built by Robert Adam in 1732, the Town House was one of Dundee's most gracious Georgian buildings. It stood on the south side of the High Street on the site of today's City Square.

CHAPTER THREE

# MOBILITY FOR THE PEOPLE

RALPH Waldo Emerson (1803-92), the American philosophic writer and essayist, averred that 'railroad iron is a magician's rod in its power to evoke the sleeping energies of land and water.' Railways, too, in the Victorian era were deemed to be symbols of 'democracy'; as the educationalist Dr Thomas Arnold (1785-1842) summed it up for all, railways were 'destroying feudality for ever'. 'Feudality' in the use of railways still had a year or two to run. On June 14th, 1842, Queen Victoria wrote to her uncle Leopold from Buckingham Palace: 'We arrived here yesterday morning, having come by the railroad, from Windsor, in half an hour, free from dust and crowd and heat, and I am quite charmed with it.' At a fare of 1/6 (7½p) the 'charm' was well beyond the pockets of the vast majority of her subjects.

By the time Victoria came to the throne the railways were already well on the way to putting coaches out of business in Dundee, and many Dundonians still travelled to London by sea. Dundee was in the forefront of railway building; for in 1831 (the year after George Stephenson opened the first English railway, between Liverpool and Manchester) the line between Dundee and Newtyle was opened. A line to Arbroath, via Broughty Ferry, was opened in 1838, to be soon followed by a rail link with Perth. By the mid-years of Victoria's reign Dundee was linked with Edinburgh and the south.

Although railways were a symbol of progress in Dundee, the railway embankment came to be a symbol of the ruthless terror of the mid-Victorian city; as well as the incredible pollution brought by the railways the new form of transport took precedence cutting swathes through the heart of the city, gobbling up houses that had been homes for centuries. The train brought many areas of Dundee and Broughty Ferry within access of working men from surrounding districts like the Fife coast, for now the time taken to get to work was drastically cut. They further made it possible to travel farther to leisure activities.

Victorian and Edwardian Dundee had traffic problems too. Wandering sheep and cattle still defied the infant rules of the road and the jam of horsedrawn drays, cabs and buses made crossing the street hazardous. Undoubtedly too, the city streets were dirtier than today with the layers of horse manure, dust from the (often unmade) surfaces, and the straw and paper from the new vogue of wrapping.

While the tram and the train contracted distance for the working man, the automobile—itself not a symbol of 'democracy' but 'status'—scattered the inhabitants pushing Dundee's boundaries farther away from its early Victorian heart. The photographs herein tell much of the joys and tragedies of the new transport systems, with a glimpse of aviation futuristics, all of which were to make the city and its surroundings a national and international talking point.

56. The Dundee Tramway and Carriage Co. Ltd, was a private one horse bus service which operated between 1877 and 1898, then it was taken over by the city authorities. Most of the early 'buses 1850-60 had no brakes and no bells.

57. Delivery cart at Bucklemakers Wynd, 1866. Bucklemakers Wynd was situated at the junction of the Wellgate and Hilltown. One of the main routes out of Dundee it was widened in 1871 and became known as Victoria Road.

58. Horse 'bus, circa 1875. Robertson's 'bus service plied between Perth Road and the Nethergate. Although in general the 'bus was a boon, it had many disadvantages in the rush hour.

59.    Dundee City Tramways, Lochee Depot, 1902. Car no 20, shown in the foreground, was a double-deck, uncanopied-open-top car built by Dick Kerr in 1900; and, was one of those supplied for the opening of the system in that year.

60.    Engine No 4 the 'Airlie'. Steam trams were introduced in 1885.

61. Tram No 59, a double-deck, extended-canopy-top-covered car, built in 1907. It had a lower top deck than others so that it could run under Barnhill Bridge.

62.    Two horse 'bus service, of the Dundee and District Tramway Co. Where possible the company tried to have one white horse and one dark horse in harness together. The Victorian and Edwardian Dundonians certainly believed that 'Advertising pays!'

63.    A **Dundee Bicycling Club of the mid-1880s. Note** their distinctive club 'uniform'. Although primitive 3-4 wheeled velocipedes had appeared in Scotland at the close of the 18th century, the earliest 2-wheeled device was that which first appeared in Paris in 1808. This gave way to the 'dandy-horse' of Kirkpatrick Macmillan, a Dumfries blacksmith, who produced a pedal-less cycle. In 1846 Gavin Dalzell, a Lesmahagow cooper, affixed pedals to Macmillan's design. The 'penny-farthing', as seen in the picture, was very popular 1880-1900; some clubs had 'duplexes'—two 'penny-farthings' coupled together.

# TAY BRIDGE DISASTER

FROM the early days of the Edinburgh-Dundee railway a huge iron paddle ferry plied the Tay from Ferryport-on-Craig to Broughty Ferry, carrying wagon trains. In 1854 Thomas Bouch, Manager and Engineer of the railway conceived the idea of building a bridge over the Tay. It took a long time to wear down opposition to the project (Perth's civic adminstrators, in particular, feared that a bridge would block navigation), but in 1871 the foundation stone was laid. In 1877 the first train crossed from Wormit, Fife, to Dundee.

Alas, because of poor workmanship and the lack of allowance for wind-pressure, a great gale struck the bridge on 28th December 1879. As the spans of the bridge collapsed a train was crossing; this plunged into the Tay at the cost of 75 lives.

In 1887 a new and more substantial bridge was built to the design of William Barlow, to become the longest bridge in the UK.

64.   The Tay Bridge from the north, looking towards Fife, before the accident. Taken in 1878.

65.    Testing the first Tay Bridge by running trial trips across it. The photograph clearly shows the wooden deck. Circa 1876.

66.    Mangled girder, Tay Bridge, 1880. The limited size of the brickwork and the poorly constructed stone piers made the whole fragile.

67.    The wreckage of the first Tay Bridge. Photograph taken 1880.

68. Locomotive 'Wheatley bogie 224' at Cowlairs after recovery following the disaster. Refitted, Locomotive 224 worked until 1924.

69. Locomotive 224's tender, fished out of the Tay.

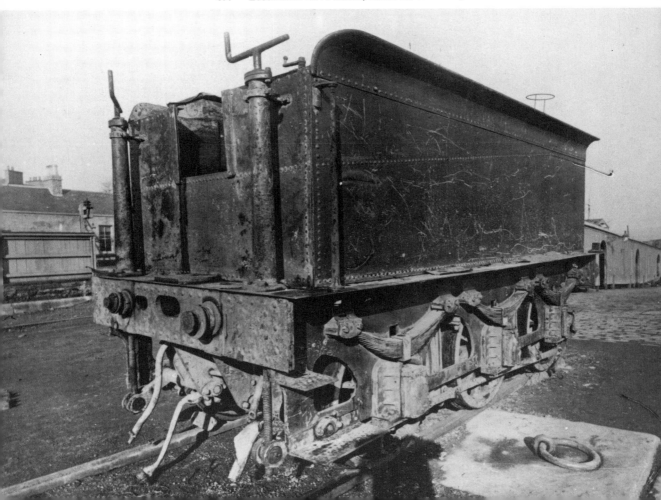

70.    Tay Bridge from the south after the accident. Note the central section of the High Girders is completely missing. 1880.

71.    Watch found on the cadaver of the guard of the passenger train which plunged into the Tay on December 28th, 1879.

72. Preston A. Watson, the Edwardian aviator taken in 1914. Watson began building a bi-plane in 1903 at Belmont, near Dundee. It was a wire and wood construction with a 10hp Santos-Daumont 2-cylinder engine. The undercarriage of the plane resembled a large pair of skis and were greased with lard. In the summer of 1903, 6 months BEFORE the Wright brothers made the first recorded flight, Watson's plane made a test flight. Hoisted by means of ropes and weights into trees, the plane was catapulted, engines running, some 100-150 yards before landing. In 1908 a second plane was built, powered by a 30hp Humber engine with a 4-wheeled undercarriage. It had a successful flight at Errol. Watson's third, and last plane, was built in 1913 and competed in open competition in Paris where its design was awarded a safety diploma. Preston Watson joined the Royal Flying Corps at the outbreak of WWI, and was killed in a training accident at Eastbourne. He was buried July 5th, 1915 in Dundee's Western Cemetery.

73.    An early flying picture. Preston Watson in flight over Errol, 1908.

74.    Preston Watson's second plane (See caption Plate 72).

CHAPTER FOUR

# CHILDREN RICH AND POOR

TO a certain extent the children of Victorian and Edwardian Dundee and Broughty Ferry were not children at all, but miniature adults. In a working-class home, where there might be as many as ten children in 2-3 rooms, they had to learn early to fend for themselves. Middleclass children too, were expected to enter the adult world of mores and godfearing morality as soon as they were weaned by the army of nannies and nurserymaids. Middleclass children saw less of their parents than their workingclass contemporaries. Washed, starched and brilliantined, and on their best behaviour, the former were allowed down from the nursery at specific hours, and stated periods of the day, to be shown off to visitors, or to converse with their parents. There was no such segregation in a tenement slum.

In dress too, the classes divided children. The sailor-suited (both sexes), crimped and laced middleclass children—the butt of urchins' jeers as they paraded to church on a Sunday, with their parents—stood out sharply against the often secondhand clothes of workingclass children. Of the very poor children, Henry Mayhew wrote: 'The rags are worn by the children as long as they will hold, or can be tied or pinned together, and when they drop off from continued wear, from dirt, and from ravages of vermin, the child sets to work to procure more.' In poorer districts of Dundee a considerable amount of cooked food was sold by street traders, and children fed themselves on pies, chips, puddings, discarded damaged fruit from the greengrocers and ice-ceam (once called 'hokey-pokey') from the pennies they earned from running 'messages'.

During the early days of Victoria's reign, small children were sacrificed in the worship of Mammon in industry. The maximum amount of work was extracted from them on the minimum of food and bedding. One form of public service conducted by children in Dundee during Victoria's early years, would be as street cleaners. Up to the 1860s children were employed (usually as freelances) to clean streets of mud, horse dung and refuse. In middleclass districts poor children were employed to shovel coal into basement storage areas, as coal was invariably dumped in the street.

Apart from a rag doll, or a wooden horse, for instance, toys were scarce in the workingclass home, yet the forms of amusement for the wealthy child were invariably touched with a modicum of instruction. Even the spelling books and story volumes were crammed with the sentiments of the day, an example being 'Cleanliness is next to Godliness.'

Leisure was seldom a problem for workingclass children, who rarely, if ever, left their back streets. Sometimes street parties were organised by the 'friendly societies' (Temperance, Sunday School Unions, Templars and so on) in which poor children were fed and patronised by their elders and betters. As long as it kept quiet, did not interfere with adult activities, and was 'decorously godly', the Victorian and Edwardian juvenile Dundonian of the well-to-do was left largely to its own devices, particularly on the occasion of a party. Yet from this seeming neglect children became the men and women who went out to rule the empire.

75.    Children at play around the fountain in the Meadows, circa 1900. Note the pinafores and summer hats.

76.    Children playing on the swings at Barrack Park circa 1899. Dudhope Castle can be seen in the background.    (overleaf)

77.　'Here Jessie, that man's put his foot in. . . Sh! He'll hear you. . . Pick up the hatbox and come on. . .' Brother and sister, 1900.

78.　Workingclass children outside a Broughty Ferry fisher cottage. Note the distinctive home-made pram and baby clothes.

79.    Children playing on the sands at Broughty Ferry. Mobile bathing machines can be seen in the background. Many of the children wear the blue and white suits which were almost compulsory seaside fashions.

80.    Adventure in his soul and pirates on his mind, a small boy gazes into space at the docks, circa 1905.

81.    Sir Francis Mudie with his sisters **Margaret and Elsie and playmate Frances Grant, 1898.** The family lived at the 'Hollies' in Holly Road and later at Yewbank (now Dundarroch), Broughty Ferry.

82.    Fisher children, many without shoes, along the shore at Broughty Ferry. Contrast their clothes and appearance with those of the Mudie children.

83.　　The Mudie children, their playmates and nannies, April 1895.

84.    Sir Francis Mudie, with his sisters Margaret and Elsie, and their governess, Mrs Epps, 1899.

85.    Harris Academy Infants' Drill, 1898. The children are playing the game 'Bluebell Fairies'.

# THE TRAINING SHIP MARS

*TTS Mars* was built as an 80-gun warship for the Royal Navy in 1848. After service in the Crimean War, the vessel was refitted as an industrial training ship. *Mars* was brought to the Tay in 1869 at the instigation of W.E. Baxter, MP for Montrose Burghs, and First Secretary of the Admiralty, and later Parliamentary Secretary. Anchored off the Fife shore at a point to the east of the Tay Bridge, *Mars* was the home for 400 boys between the ages of 12 and 16. On board they were given a basic education, with training in seamanship, woodwork and tailoring. Emphasis too, was placed on rowing, boxing, swimming and gymnastics. Many of the boys came to the *Mars* on a naval scholarship to learn the basics of a career at sea, while others were there because they were orphaned or homeless, or had committed civil misdemeanours or persistent truancy. In all some 7000 boys passed through training on the *Mars*, but by 1929 numbers had fallen off. She was then towed to Inverkeithing for breaking. So thick were some of the timbers of the *Mars* that she had to be dynamited. The *Mars* was also known for its choir and band.

86.     The *Mars* boys being rowed ashore at Woodhaven. This boat carried visitors to and from the *Mars*, and acted as a rescue vessel for the Tay.

87.　*Mars* boys in the woodwork workshops. They made a variety of goods ranging from toys, stools and tables to the most delicate inlaid boxes. The work was sold to the public and helped finance the running of the ship. Notice that the boys' heads have been shaven as a measure against lice.

88. The *Mars* rowing boat. Boat crews were appointed on a weekly basis and their duties included rowing post and supplies to and from the shore.

89. Gymnastics on the Newport-Tayport railway embankment. Great emphasis was placed on sport; the boys had no choice in the matter and were made to take part. This was a favourite postcard-greetings card pose of the early 1900s.

# CHAPTER FIVE

# DUNDEE FACES

90. These men, probably itinerant preachers, were photographed outside the Albert Institute, circa 1900. The Meadows area was a popular place for street oratory. One preacher carries the gospels while the other carries the preaching stool.

91.   A Broughty Ferry fisherwoman baiting fishing lines. This job was traditionally performed by women. Baiting the
hundreds of hooks often took hours, and unmarried men were generally forced to pay for having their lines baited.

92.  'Och Charlie, that's an awfy length y'er goin' for a toffee.'
     'Naw, naw man. My teeth were stuck tae it.'
     (Note the workman's 'bus on the bridge.)

93. The Fine Art Committee of the British Association at its 1867 annual meeting held in Dundee. Left to right: William Small, P. Anderson, Thomas Robertson, William Ritchie, Bishop Forbes, J.C. Bell, Alexander Scott, John Leng, J. Henderson, G.B. Simpson, J.G. Orchar, P.G. Walker, and Lord Kinnaird. Many famous people visited the city during the conference including the inventor Sir David Brewster (see page 19), and the mother of the poet Keats. The conference was marked by the switching on of the first electric light in Dundee, outside the High School in September 1867.

94. Graduates from University College, Dundee, 1909-1910. Compare these faces with those of Plate 105.

95.    A Sunday promenade, circa 1905, showing two interesting examples of fashions for women. Such fashions were called 'walking-out ensembles'.

96.  A delightful conversation piece of 1899. The 'wasp-waist' was still fashionable for women up to the 1900s. From the 1860s, home dressmaking was given a boost by the appearance of the hand-cranked sewing-machine at a guinea (£1.05p).

97. Jute merchants discuss prices outside the Jute Shelter in the Meadows, circa 1900.

98. A delightful informal study of browsers at the Greenmarket, in the 1880s.

99.   Fashionable Dundee ladies of the turn of the century. Middle-class fashions reflected the stiffness and formality of the middle-class mind. The tram, which is standing outside the old Post Office (today the 'Courier' building) is running on the first tram route in Dundee—from the Post Office to Sinderins—established 1877.

100. Passers by stare at a photographer in the Meadows about 1900. Since the Stone Age, furs have been fashionable for women. Their range in Victorian and Edwardian Dundee and Broughty Ferry included such forgotten apparel as muffs, dolmans, paletots and pelisses.

101. Dundonians loiter behind the Burns statue in the Meadows, 1899.

102. With whisky at 1/4d a bottle, life was good for some; the face of this prosperous Gentleman radiates his joy with life.

103.  The staff of Ancrum Road School, Dundee, 1911.
*Back row:* Miss Wood; Mr. Moncrieff; Miss Wilson; Miss Mackenzie; Mr. Cape; Miss Grant; Miss Smith;
Miss Mitchell.
*Second row:* Miss Ogilvie; Miss Ramsay; Mr. Neill; Miss Philip; Miss Elder; Miss Brebner.
*Third row:* Miss Sadler; Miss Macmillan; Miss Bell; Mr. Locke; Miss Stewart; Miss Wedderspoon; Miss Stewart.
*Front row:* Miss Morrison; Miss Macdonald.

The Education Act of 1870 put an end to the few private academies of a Dickensian nature which still existed. By
1900 standards of teaching and discipline had much improved.

104.  David Brown Livie a competitor in the Leng Crystal Claret Cup single sculls, July 1875. Born February 24th, 1847, in St Margaret's Close, Fish Street, Dundee, he was the son of David Livie the boatbuilder. For much of the 19th century D. Livie & Sons was an important firm in Dundee, building boats ranging from rowing boats to whalers.

105.  The Dundee Old Steeple Bellringing Society, 1880. Compare these humourless, blank, characterless faces with the eager, well-fed, bright expressions in the Plate 94 group.

106. Mary Slessor, pictured here on a visit to Scotland in 1898, with some of the twin-children she saved.

★　　★　　★　　★　　★

Mary Slessor was born at Aberdeen on December 2nd, 1848. She was 11 years old when she moved to Dundee where she worked at Baxter's Mill as a '½-timer'. Deeply religious, Mary was a regular attender at the Wishart Church. In 1875, she offered her services to the Foreign Mission Committee as a missionary. On August 5th, 1876, she sailed from Liverpool to the Calabar region of Nigeria. She taught day school and dispensed medicines. As well as preaching Christianity, Mary Slessor battled against local superstitious customs, one of which was enforced murder of twin babies.

She died on January 13th, 1915, at Akpap and was buried at Duke Town.

107.   Mary Slessor and her household at Okoyong, Nigeria. Mary moved through many areas of Nigeria setting up mission schools, converting people to Christianity and acting as a judge in local disputes.

# CHAPTER SIX

# DOWN HIGHWAYS AND BYWAYS

'OUR age is pre-eminently the age of great cities' wrote Robert Vaughan in his *The Age of Great Cities* (1843). Dundee was to take its place in Victorian Scotland as symbolic of the fashions of the age from its new street lighting and commercial façades, to its cobblestones and clanking tramways. The taste of the early Victorians was undoubtedly for the romantic and for moral inspiration with exaggerated delicacy of feeling. It was the era of the Gothic Revival, that drawn out architectural experiment which incorporated the Victorian appeal for the romantic; and, it appeared in various forms in Victorian Dundee to give the city new sights down highway and byway.

The influence of the Gothic Revival was first seen on church architecture, and in time it spread to all forms of the art. The Victorians in particular—for the Revival had really begun in the late 1700s—were inspired to their architectural excesses by a hazy belief that Gothic buildings and environs helped to induce a return of all that was best in medieval life, from worship to chivalry.

Because of this the architects of Victorian and Edwardian Dundee and Broughty Ferry turned railway stations into Gothic cathedrals, banks and offices into Florentine *palazzi* look-alikes; and, all around artists and artisans were encouraged to look backwards in time for inspiration. This trend was to prevail up to the early 1900s when Victorian pretence and opulence took on some Edwardian elegance and extravagance first seen in Angus, perhaps, in the new house of the wealthy at Broughty Ferry and in Dundee's Perth Road.

In the 1880s a shroud of scaffolding fell over Victorian Dundee and the mock-baronial of Broughty Ferry. Yet, between the new buildings, of course were the gloomy, squalid and insanitary dwellings of the workingclass, with the innumerable courts and closes. There was a mid-Victorian movement towards demolishing the old houses, but the attitude of mind that bred and tolerated such slums was not demolished, so that the mean and filthy conditions in which many hundreds of Dundonians lived remained throughout the period.

Of all that the descendants of Queen Victoria were to inherit for good or evil, nothing was to be more influential or destructive to the highways and byways than the combusion engine. The complicated, and often hideous, vehicles emphasised the dichotomy that grew between commerce and culture, contrary to all that Albert the Prince Consort had had in mind when he worked hard on the Great Exhibition of 1851.

Victorian Dundee produced its own sounds and scents. In the streets, the smell of leather, horses and sawdust mingled with the aroma of ground coffee and the broth and braziers of the street food sellers. The jingle of horse harness, the ring of hooves on cobbles and the clatter of steel-rimmed wheels, blended with the street-cries of the tradesmen, the clack of hobnailed boots on pavement and the jangle of the delivery carts. The coming of the evil-smelling petrol engine was to kill the old smells of commerce and muffle in its progress the wholesome sounds of yesteryear.

108. The High Street, Dundee on a market day in 1875. Markets were held on Tuesdays and Fridays, and were popular with Dundee businessmen who liked to stroll up and down the High Street. The horses and carriages of the cab rank, which always stood outside the Town House, can be seen on the right.

109.   The High Street, Dundee, 1890-95. The demolition of the Trades Hall has revealed the Clydesdale Bank and opened the entrance to the Seagait and Murraygate. Smith Bros have opened a large drapery emporium at No. 4, next to Tyndal's Wynd.

110. The Overgate, 1895. Franchi's *confiseri* was one of the many Italian firms found in Dundee's catering trade.

111. The Murraygate, circa 1890. The carbon lamps in the centre of the foreground and the lamp pillars are still in existence.

112.   High Street, 1898. Fleming & Haxton, shipping agents, were still at No. 44 High Street. This was taken shortly before
their move to No. 76.

113. **Strathtay House on the corner of Reform Street and the Old Overgate, circa 1900.** Strathtay House were the premises of Adam Smail 'boys , and youths' clothier, girls' costumier and gentlemen's outfitter' from the early 1870s. After the death of Adam Smail, it was run under the same name by trustees up to WWI, when it was taken over by the Manfield Boot and Shoe Co, and is today Boots the Chemists.

114.  Overgate looking towards the High Street and City Square with the Episcopal Church in the background, circa 1890.
The first turning on the right is Thorter Row, which joined the Overgate and Nethergate and was said to be the
smallest street in Dundee.

115. The Greenmarket which was situated at the foot of Crichton Street, and the junction of Shore Terrace. Markets were held here chiefly on Fridays and Saturdays. The stalls boasted sweets, flowers, fish, meat, all kinds of foods, among which stood fiddlers, pickpockets, organ grinders, whores, auctioneers and street preachers.

116. Water Wynd before the building of Victoria Road in 1872. The road on the left leads into Bell Street. The building on the corner is the United Presbyterian Church.

117. Carmichael's Wine Bar in the Vault. The Vault was behind the Old Town House on the site of today's City Square, it connected the High Street and the Greenmarket.

118. **The Meadows, originally a** common grazing area, was built over in the 1850s.
The Congregational Church, on the corner of Panmure Street and Euclid Crescent, was built in 1855, and the Royal Exchange was constructed in 1853. The low building in the middle is the Jute Shelter which was the hub of Dundee's jute industry, where jute was bought and sold.

119. Dundee's skyline, 1910. The relationship between the city and the docks is clearly seen.

120.   A bustle of pedestrians and tradesmen outside the High School, about 1900. A delivery boy rests with his barrow.

# CHAPTER SEVEN

# SHIPS AND THE SEA

DUNDEE is used to seeing both ships of commerce and war. For instance, in 1040 the vessels of King Malcolm (Canmore) anchored here when they were in pursuit of Macbeth. A free harbour was granted to the burghers of Dundee by William the Lion at the turn of the 12th and 13th centuries, a right confirmed by Robert Bruce. Thus the harbour of Dundee was an important strategic position, a fact not lost on Scotland's enemies down the centuries, who gave Dundonians many a 'naval incident' to witness.

Just before Victoria came to the throne Dundee harbour was becoming inadequate so a Bill for the Improvement of the Harbour was passed. The laying of the foundation stone for the 'extensive new works', as the historian and public librarian A.H. Miller described them, took place on October 13th, 1815.

Writing in1912, J.H. Martin averred: 'It may be said that physically the City's best asset lies in the fact that she is a seaport. There is regular communication by sea with all the great ports in England and Ireland, and many on the Continent, while the great jute-laden vessels from India form a yearly argosy far exceeding in value and importance those of Ragusa and Venice. At present everything points to a further development of the resources of the port. In this way the volume of overseas trade may be expected to increase and new interest aroused in connection with the shipbuilding industry. Some years ago Dundee Harbour was created a Naval Base and the waters of the Tay utilised as an anchorage for submarine craft.'

Dundee long has had connections with the Royal Navy, supplying several 'famous sons of the sea', like Admiral Adam Duncan (b. 1731), Commander-in-Chief of the North Sea Fleet. A submarine base was established at Dundee and the King William and the Graving Docks were used for mooring, repair and overhaul of RN craft. In Edwardian times, the 6620-ton RN ship *H.M.S. Vulcan* was a common sight moored off the Fife shore near Newport—all familiarising Dundonians with naval affairs and naval methods. Dundee was one of the trio of ports which formed the Scottish home of the Royal Naval Volunteer Reserve (established 1913), Clyde Division. A branch of the Navy League was established in Dundee in 1898. Politically Dundee had a strong representation on the Board of Admiralty. Edmund Robertson, one of the MPs for Dundee, had a seat on the Board and in 1908 became Parliamentary and Financial Secretary to the Admiralty. The Rt. Hon. Winston S. Churchill, Member for Dundee was the First Lord of the Admiralty, 1911-15.

All in all ships and the sea brought great wealth and fame to Dundee. Much of the canvas used in the Royal and Merchant navies (particularly during Victorian and Edwardian times) was made by Baxter Bros & Co. Ltd., Dens Road.

121. The *Bonnie Dundee* leaving Broughty Pier. Pleasure steamers were a common sight in Victorian and Edwardian times, with trips running from Dundee to Newburgh and Perth. A service also took in May Island and the Bell Rock, with trips to Montrose and Arbroath.

122.   The Submarine Miners' steamer *Sir William Reid* off Broughty Ferry in the 1890s.

123.   *The Carlyle*, a pleasure steamer bought by the Tay Steamboat Co. in 1909. Subsequently the vessel was sold to the Admiralty in 1915.

124. **Sprat yawls in Dundee Harbour. The boat in the foreground shows its registration number clearly, DE (Dundee), No 156.**

125. *S.V. Lawhill* built by the Caledon Shipyard in 1892 for Charles Barrie, who ran one of the most successful jute shipping firms in Dundee. Barrie was a great believer in sailing ships and the *Lawhill*, one of the last of the windjammers, proved herself by remaining in service up to the 1920s.

126. A Dundee whaler stands proudly, ensign flapping, in the North Sea sometime in the 1890s.

127. 'Come to grief', the sad end of another whaler around 1895.

128.   Fishing boats beached at Broughty Ferry, around 1900.

129.   Paddle steamers and fishing boats in the King William IV dock.

130. Shipping moored in the west part of King William IV dock. This area is now filled in, but the Telford lighthouse on the right of the picture still stands incorporated into the gardens of the waterfront.

131.
The 90 ton steam crane was installed in the Victoria dock in 1875 when the dock was first opened. It was used for bunkering coal for steamers, lifting bulky machinery and a multitude of heavy work.

132.
A view of Dundee Harbour, Earl Gray Docks. The rail tracks which ran along the harbour edge are visible. Sand boats pulled into the docks and off-loaded directly into rail trucks.

133.   The Tidal basin, Dundee Docks, looking towards the Royal Arch, circa 1893.

134.   The entrance lockway to the Earl Gray Dock, and the Dockmaster's office. Circa 1890.

135. *Discovery* dipping her ensign.

## DISCOVERY

Built by the Dundee Shipbuilders Co. Ltd, largely at the instigation of Sir Clements Markham, President of the Royal Geographical Society for an expedition to the Antarctic, led by Captain R.F. Scott, *Discovery* was designed by Sir William White, a Senior Ships Constructor at the Admiralty. She was launched on March 21st, 1901, from the old Stephens Yard, from which so many of the city's whaling fleet had first entered the water. After trials on the Tay, *Discovery* sailed south leaving Spithead on August 6th, bound for New Zealand. A leak, the 'Dundee Leak', was discovered on the voyage and a great deal of heated discussion took place over it between the constructors and Markham. She left Lyttleton on Christmas Eve 1901, eventually returning there on April 2nd, 1904, after two winters in the Antarctic ice. After Scott's expedition, *Discovery* saw service with the Hudson Bay Company becoming a Royal Research Ship in 1923. 1929 again saw her in the Antarctic with Sir Douglas Mawson's Australia Expedition. In 1936 she was moored on the Thames Embankment where she was used by the Boy Scouts Association, RNVR and the Royal Navy before being acquired for preservation by the Maritime Trust in 1978. She is to be restored to her 1925 configuration and is, at present, to be seen in St. Katherine's Dock, London.

136. On the deck of *Discovery*: the men stand by the double wheel showing the 'kicking brake'.

137. *Discovery* leaving dock, after her offical launch.

138.  *Discovery* running the 'measured mile' while on sea-trials. The ship's performance was assessed during this; a 'nautical mile' being one minute of a great circle of the earth, fixed by the British Admiralty at 6080 feet.

139. *Discovery* successfuly pursues her trials.

140.  Pleasure craft at West Ferry, circa 1900.

141.   'The short and the tall'; small fishing boats and large jute ships in Dundee harbour, around 1895.